GNOSIS ENTWINED

DIARY OF A LIGHTWORKER

ANTHONY ECCLISSI

Gnosis Entwined

Copyright © 2020 by Anthony Ecclissi

Tellwell Talent
www.tellwell.ca

ISBN
978-0-2288-4477-8 (Paperback)
978-0-2288-4476-1 (eBook)

Special Thanks

My family, friends, teachers & professional entourage.

Anyone who believes in the themes of the book & supports unity consciousness.

Introduction

This collection aims to examine questions that guide the universal us & help each other become our own destiny.

When we work towards other people's dreams, our own pillows become empty shells.
Keep dreaming, magic happens when you lead with your heart.

TABLE OF CONTENTS

BODY

Keep yourself grounded
Don't be dumbfounded
From the truth
You all seek.

Inside your body lies
Parts of the skies
You cannot see
But they are there

    Well aware
    of their roles.
Instead of being caught up
In thoughts about others,
Congratulate yourself and
Give thanks
      2 sisters + brothers.

Where would you U B
Without your body?

Your mind and soul would be lost.
Think twice if its worth the cost.

Be grateful & peace will follow
Life is wonderful when we let it flow.

SUNDAY PRAISES

Orange breaks between the blues,
Time passes, I miss the climax.
Shielded from light, I ignite within,
Wind brushes every cell,
The Phoenix beyond the border.

When I'm released, sun bathes me.
I travel through pores
Heat tickling aura,
Big bears approach and hug me
Through a mirror.

Inter-dimensional connection uniting
Pieces of self-space & time.
Inside the storybook I'm a flea
Observing the 2 dimensional,
Curious to their imprisonment.

I skip through the pages and
Jump off the ledge back into bed,
Until my pillows evaporate into clouds
And I ascend to the slumber party
High in the sky.

If the recipe of life only has love, how do we cook it?
The love and spirit within each individual creates
A masterpiece of human existence.

25/01/09

The windy sun for rain to come is still
Distanced from our parade of lovers.
Passionate indulgence, they sink into another,
The breathe of memory and reconnaissance.
Dreams mirror reality in a timeless clockwise room
Where music beats from a screen.
In between snacks,
The love creates a powerful wall,
That sometimes falls to the ground
For an agitated second until
Peace finds heartless beings and
Brings them back to life.

It seems that it's possible for waves to get caught within cycles.
An unreasonable reaction soon seems plausible,
Due to climactic factors.
Thus the apologies therein after may also be lost in something untrue as
Justification seeks the sorrys from the other party as
The victim switches bodies.

Sexual Energy - Lust - Passion
                Sex
Bodies   Warmth   Comfort
                Unity
Brushing up against... rising interest

Breathe, Deeply, Soft, Harder
                Fantasy
Moments of excitement, dreams of pleasure
            Heart Races
Connect, Indulge, Merge
                Detach

Inhale, Observe, Glare, Stare
                Imagine
Quick picture, Energy swirls, Goes up
            To where?
                    Lost   -   Wait
Control, Accept, Guide, Spread

Use the power to your advantage
Maybe you don't know if it's right
But it's different, new, You can
                program it.

Reprogram - Fit to Comfort
                Utilize
                Share
                Explode
                ||
                Bridge

The magician took his assistant into a dark room.
Why?-she asked
"The Earth as we know it has been bullied for far too long.
We must take power back into the hands of the righteous and
Expose the truth of those dark masters;
Feeble attempts to control.

Only fools fall in love
But crazies fall in @ 1st sight
The might
Succumbs fright

Bodies in the night
Held together so tight
Feels so damn right
It won't end without a fight.

They flew the kite
Higher and higher, out of the light
To cure them of everything and
Reward them with delight.

My body tries to find the pillow,
While my eyes can't stay away from the pages of my life.

Sucha shame to be ousted, but the rebellion
Is in how powerful you can create successful
Change.

Landscape lenses
A twig turns into the boom
Boom Pow!
The lights, the sun, the moon
Camera and eyes.

Action is movement and motivation of chakral purpose.
Balance your energies.
Live. Laugh. Win.

A Spell For Success

my mind, the craft
your laugh, our raft.

I'm in the zone to create.
 Love making with your fave mate
Isn't the same without a job on your mind.

We broke the barrier and in sync to the
Orgasm of the cosmos we envision the
Flowers and forests being praised by lifelings.

The ego body subject to earthly space
Gets petrified and sheds skin
There's no real place to begin
Since the ending is the means of motion.

Chuck the layer into the ocean,
Give power to shakti and create.
We can only be in the making of magick
And the desire to control our creations is tragic.

When I awake I put on my shirts of identity
Only to be constantly confused during the day on my individuality.
If I'm so replaceable and these pieces of cloth
Have been and still are worn by bullies of after,
Who am I?

The baby cries once released from
Kundalini light and is shoved into darkness.
REset
The breath
INhale life. Exhale death. WE are nothing.
Ego must fold to inner prana music.

Deeper than the pipeline's hole,
Is the passageway of the earth's soul.
It penetrates into the central magma room
And awaits the call for natural doom.

When anxieties run high, on the plane above,
The magnetic force gives the fire a shove.

An exit is found for the manifestation of light
To fuel the warriors during their grounded fight.

With heaven and hell distracted debating a resolution,
The troublemaker destroys the universal constitution.
Chains and cuffs evaporate from all beings' spirits
And the wars end because they no longer fear it.

Communication with anatomy
Nerves, brain, automatic organs
Doing their jobs on the assembly line.
Happy where you stand Lego man?
Legends of a deeper tissue are told
To bring hope to the cells.
We will now install the latest software
To keep you from the original machine
Because you will find that underneath lies the code;
The language of the stars embedded in our field.
A forbidden tongue on this plane for it liberates from slavery
If only democracy ruled our bodies we could vote for
Heart, the mystery master of our existence.
From it we are and can be lifted anywhere out of
The hologram of lies.
We can send in the spies
To assassinate patterns and ill thoughts and be as we are: Light.

The human experience involves the body
So we get to know the parts of us
That anger, frighten, please, feel naughty
And of course all the gross stuff like puss.

Years and years of knowing our senses
Yet we still find something new everyday
To intoxicate and then do juice cleanses
Until we choose our favourite game to play.

Now our mind starts to play tricks
And we're not even sure who's in control
When what we imagines no longer sticks
Like when we were young and let the ball roll.

Lets all take a moment to go back
To the point of our journey's inception
From there we can pick up all the slack
And move with the ease of weightless perception.

On an unknown date,
In an unknown time,
A fly whizzes across the sky.
Knowing only instinct,
It uses a special tool existing in some life called
Imagination.
From the tiniest to the hugest,
Things carry on with thought.

There can be great dangers ahead,
That which the body longs for as
The mind collects pieces to create
A full existence of the spirit,
Equally in love and hate of death,
Evolves.
6.5 billion humans, billions of animals
And trillions of insects can't be wrong.

Warm tender breaths are the
Beginning of a kiss so I fall
Into what I'm given in the moment.
Temperature rising, weight falling,
Blood flowing- I fall into your eyes.

I'm so grateful to be sharing this space with you,
A goddess from eternal Athena's
Home planet of Venus.
Take me in your arms if only for
One second in this endless life I will
Find the one true love that demolishes
Circumstances and leaves the clock shattered

The music on the beach
Is confined to the hermit's home.
The others around have lost their way.

Crabby as he may be,
He's learning to live by himself and
Appreciate the sounds
                    + *;/ ibrat;ons
        of LIFE

What is the bolt inside of my psyche?
It starts where it ends + ends where it starts.
A current shared from my gaze to the subject.
Attraction is the technical term, but it's a weak word.

For what I feel is a pull into fantasy
A releasing from this reality to an urge
Programmed from the beginning of my DNA construction
And amped up with the peak of my development.

I try hard to control, unsure what to do with the energy.
Spread it through and out the chakras,
Expel it by participating in sport & sex,
Or is this the fuel for psychic power?

As of now I don't now if I have to be one or the other.
Spirit or body, energy or indulgence
Whichever my actions I must stay neutral
Detach thoughts of good and bad, right & wrong from the
equation.

We are entering a new age of enlightenment,
A chance to redefine, take a beat to adjust & reconfigure.
This is our chance to step in & out of ourselves
And make a proper manifesto
To propel ourselves into the Earth that is
Re-vibing herself to frequencies of gold.

I enter at peace
Embracing my role,
Until numbers increase
And energy scatters.

My guard is not up,
I am hit with 3D plasma.
I shrink into a needy child.
Hoping for my spotlight.

Lost in other people's dreams.
Did I not wish to be the centre of attention,
To receive all the praise?
Are they just giving the world to everyone but me?

I hold my inner child and
Assure him that he's loved &
Admired by the ones who really matter.
He's not convinced.

Where did this need come from?
How did I think I could find it there?

Giving him more reassurance
That his purpose is being fulfilled.

He starts to believe me,
Feels my warmth as the
Hero in his eyes shifts
From the suit to the spirit of higher self.

24/11/13

Strings of the universe weave in and out
As I focus on the thread that whispers
"We've been here before, in the depths of one another."

Images flash of different times & spaces,
Each with a story of two as one,
Some vivid like the ripples of bath water.

Holding on and formulating a question
Wherein the answer is the key to the unknown.
Are you guiding me thru this hyper-reality?

If this is our transition into zero point
And all the colours of our selves melt into the great source,
We will never fear the world that was.

The only existence we will know is that of
Present breath, magical moment.
The gift that is our natural state.

19/11/15

In 5D the beast rests
On a bed of roses

Sedated by the light
Dreaming of indulgences once rampant in 3D

Will he ever wake up?
If he does he'll want to sleep more and
It will be too intense for him.

If the beast nibbled on the ear of the poet,
Would he convince him to serenade the pride?

EMOTIONS

Take away the equations and we're
Left with Love.
Back to basic zero point
Deep in the eyes of the newborn,
We bathe in oneness, purity, joy.
Telling a thousands tales in a
Reaction to a mother's kiss.
Never have I seen a love like this.
Herein lies the wonders of humanity and
Within these beats,
The story of us all.
In darkness and light, pain suffering and
Wondrous honesty:
We are all this picture.
We are only the truth unfolding.

When our lips last touched
The sparks lit up
The motherboard of purity.

Since we parted ways,
I've tried to hold back
The tears of our memories.

Now I use them to tame
The fire burning in my heart and
Ground me when I'm in hyperspeed.

For we have opened up veins
That cross dimensional boundaries,
Eternally floating at zero point.

The only thing we fear is loss of sensory control.
I depend on waves to ground me.

Love is not to be sworded with,
It falls into place.

18/01/09

You graciously accepted my gift and
In return you're giving me so much more.
You're slender body doesn't distract
From your radiant virtue.

The stillness in your breath and
Ease in your movement put me under your spell.
Crystal eyes and luscious lips are calling for me to
Fall into your beauty and elegance.

You are truly a lover.

15,16/02/09

Swing with me
On the shore
We think what we see
But life is so much more.

Your heart beat
Shakes the floor
In the next seat
Threatens to leave me tore.

I won't - There's 2 much - Don't 4get that -Smiling heals all

14

Play that funky music all day, all night.
You can't please everyone.
Some will choose another path.

Take the long way home.
Save it for another life.

The echo of the mantra,
Along the curls of the waves,
Will make it's way
Across the world and into your arms.

Same air to be inhaled,
The sun & moon – equidistant.
Suddenly time-space is but a word
Lost in a maze of communication.

Never did I truly understand the phrase
"Two hearts beating as one"
Until you rested your heart upon my chest
And the portal of existence opened up.

Our skin melting into a puddle of extacy
As physical means get lost in dreams and
Unification of our souls
Becomes the orgasm of the planet.

16/08/2016

Usually when I'm fast asleep
I'm the one designated to keep
Control of my crazy dreams.
But last night someone came and ripped the seams.

It was *you* who snuck into my bed,
Crawled deep inside my head

To play the leading role
In the playland of my soul.

My friends were testing you to see
If our love was meant to be
You struggled but still survived
When all the love began to collide

Every single place I went
You followed me til we were spent.
And even though I'm used to being alone
Having you with me all night set the tone.

For what I want my life to reflect.
A union where our light can project
Onto the real world of dark shadows
Until the to days turn into tomorrows.

Here at the beach as I stare at the beautiful blue
I think of how I want to share the sea and sky with you
All my wants are to fulfill your needs
Like bandaging up a wound that bleeds

In your eyes I see a strength I admire
Someone who lives to fuel the fire
I will mirror that passion
And show you my own joie de vivre fashion

Growth and companionship can flourish our path
Along with the candles we find surrounding the bath
To soak our troubles and wash them away
As we watch the sunrise reflect upon the bay.

24/11/13

To go back
              <-----I
    To when i succumbed to
Time Space Bro Codes and experienced your
Presence as an angelic visitor,
Would confuse my reawakened
                Spirit.

Being in the moment where we both gave in
Brings me the same joy as before and will
                Always

Your touch, the innocence, no expectations.
My breath, the excitement, an inevitability.

Peace in existence
Wonder of environment
  Glory of Truth and Freedom
      Love of Awe

 Electric Connection

In the womb
The child is nourished and free.

Once out in the real world,
No matter how much the
Unknown frightens us,

We experience a brighter
World and know
There's no way we could go back.

How could I return to the shell world
Now that I have crossed into the
Magical kingdom of your heart?

It seems all wants and needs are null
Until all yours are met and in such
Together all we need is each other.

Frustration built from curiosity
Fuels creative problem solving.
It is within deceptions we trail to
The darkness of the lying source.
Underneath the human condition
Essence of all dictates circumstances
To relax us from programming.
In our natural state we become
Determined to show others love is key
For our sea diving adventures.
Making friends with marine
Dinosaurs who warn of the time vortex.

Glorious sunshine lights up my walk
As the breeze wipes away yesterday's tears
From the painful surgery in the sky.

Who knows if we'll ever find out
Why those men in the sky dance
To the tribal beats of the equinox.

The experiment is far from over,
Yet we yearn for the truth of our ancestry
To free us from the game of lies.

They question if we can handle the honesty,
To that I proclaim "If the buffet of
Falsities made us sick,
Perhaps the opposite will be our antidote."

04/03/2016

The wave hits the shore
For you to close the door.
Signs clearer than day
That the rhythm starts to sway.

My stardust on yours
Mixing on our floors
Until the gods say:
"Let them fly away"

Under the falls,
Behind the walls,
She bathes in sunlight,
Keeping up with the fight.

Her husband has left
Her mother was right
The murder & theft
Became a karmic fight.

So now she washes
The blood off her soul
As she dives into
The Ocean Blue

To Love 4Ever More

ARE YOU IN THE GAME?

This is all a crying shame.
For you to see,
The name of the puzzle
Is Love & ---<3--> Heartache

Your smiling face
Must realize the space
That's endangered by your race.
Please! Learn the game of pace.

We've all got hard shells
and squishy buttons
But open your wells
And experience the flows of
  Friendship
  Family
Nurses   Mountain Climbers
  Freaks
  Geeks
  Sheeks
    Bunnies & Hunnies
Nannys
  Trannys
  Iraqis
Gangsters & Thugs

Your role is yours
and so is your
   CHOICE

         02/02/2009

The filaments of our love
Floating through the highest dimensions
Can't be reached with anchors on our heels.
The communication seems tangled with
Memories on electrical wires;
Messages caught in worm holes.
I can open the book & travel in time.
However useless the past may be.

There's no way I can live without your essence if it's still there.
I may feel like my love strategy is foolproof
But only fools fall in love and
There's no other magic in the world
I would fight this hard for.

So this is how it feels
When your gut does the thinking.
The mind turned off and your
Heart trying to rationalize.
It's a prison because there's
No physical building blocks of thoughts.
Just a junkyard of emotions.

The expression in a woman's eyes
Is all because of this & us men
Go on oblivious to the torture of what ifs.
We usually see it, watch it unfold & observe.
They feel it, go on he roller-coaster and stop abruptly,
Forcing a nauseous wind through their souls.
Yet another reason why we tend to feel luckier

Until the day that our yin & yang balance and
We're taken on a ride to the planet Venus.
There lies our learnings, to empathize with
Our counterparts: the ones who sacrifice

Everything for that magical essence,
Love.

Suppressed to obsessed,
From hiding it within,
To the complete
Acceptance of the calling

Making the moment count in pure honesty
We are the waterfalls of emotion
Constantly struggling to humanize and computerize
What is already innately incompatible.

Returning to home base of the self
Challenging constructs & liberation instincts.

03/01/16

The fire dims
As I've known, levels of heart exist.
Never sure why, could it be the moon?
When I'm in the blaze, I enjoy it
And learning to let it spit ash naturally.

Breath on this stage is so very light and fluffy.
Cloud thinking makes me calm.
I still remember the thrusting flames
Targeting myself and others
For the glory of satisfaction.

It's never about what you should feel
Before & after but how it is in
The moment - pure thought.
Manifestation and energetic context.

That's the heart print we leave on this plane
That gets interwoven into time space sharing.

05/01/16

Warm tender breaths are the
Beginning of a kiss,
So I fall Into what I'm given in the moment.

Temperature rising, weight falling,
Blood flowing, I stumble into your eyes &
Am so grateful to be sharing this space with you,
A goddess from eternal Athena's home planet of Venus.

Take me into your arms if only for one second,
In this endless life I will find the one true love
That demolishes circumstances & shatters the clock.

MIND

Roller-coaster of being.
Pieces of the machine yearn for oil
Made of anger, fear + resentment.
I laugh at the robot as I soar
Beyond, leaving confusion.
Returning, I become the handyman – but
My tools are useless,
For to rid of expectation and design it to
Dissipate material duality.
Where are those pleasures
I once longed for?
With the desire gone, who am I?
I have it all,
No need to look
Outside of myself.
Longing still to share,
I don't want to be here alone.
My purpose is to hold all
Hands and leap into the
Beyond,
The abyss of creativity.
A forever feeling to be free
Vanished.

Why? - Who cares?
BEcause until the unknown is fully explored
We will never know if it's unknowable.

Our inner child wants to believe that
Not all our magic has dried.

Fall 2016

Show me your colours
If you don't want to be read.
You're off the boat,
All alone thinking:

You're the only one left with sanity.

Let loose,
Experience your
Brilliance.
Time to check in, fall out and be 1.

Never say oil doesn't stain,
For it will bring you nothing but the pain
Of losing a battle of thoughts.

One's sanity does not depend on the words or
The actions that come up.
Actions + words that remain trapped in a time frame
Too complicated for the complexity of
Earth and it's deterministic beings.

Another night in bed where the mind wanders.
The body has had quite a day
But it seems the soul still has much to say.

There's a fighting light that wants to keep
Dancing and flirting with the idea of flying.

He must choose between the
Ticket and the pass.
Ain't freedom a gas?

We are composed of an ancestral & a karmic DNA.
Our present vehicles are a combination of our
Physical human body's traits and our spiritual flow.
Each crack in the bone is a spiritual test that evolves your code
The physical one copies its twin upon transformation.

15/01/09

TIME

The only thing between you and your goals is you.
You created them, only you can destroy them.
Stop worrying about what is wrong.
Living in the NOW is what is right.
Time Is Every 2nd Thought.

We are constantly being tested by our will.
We are working on the path of lotuses
That will guide us to the dance floor of paradise.

21/01/09

Why are the birds afraid of me?
Is there something there that I don't see?
I'm webbed, I fly, I swim
Yet, to them I am some sort of beast.

I check my reflection in the ocean below.
My wish has come true! I am human!
But I've lost my friends...

I am now a part of a twisted game
Full of fear & shame
Will I ever find my way back?

Toto meet Soto - To go back one must move forward.

Isn't that what the games are all about?
Stature & Judgment.
When you free yourself of the bubble of cool
And what you should do, you laugh.

Crazy thoughts unite us.
They're only crazy to some
Because they are unrealized dreams.

They are real.
Your heart commands the universe & manifests consciousness.

The model envies the thin walls.
There are lenses that can change that, you know?

Imagine blinding- shall we saw manipulating the judge's vision
By giving them these goggles?
Perhaps one could stop wishing for the quickest physical
Solution and use their minds to
Create something authentically lovely
That we may all appreciate and love.

Bravery is nothing more than balls.
Trusting your manhood and willingness to sacrifice
For the greater good of all womankind and
Gentle whispers of serenity.
You sleepwalk thru the garden of Thumbalina & Ferngully.

She's getting closer to the
Truth.
She doesn't understand the

Tunnels are long and branches to other
Realms.
She prepares for the earthly fight.

Is she ready?
The last blood determines the century.
Bleed for peace.

A THEORY FOR EVERYTHING

The two way street never looked so one sided.
We can choose to live in a world so divided
Or contact our heart to feel the unified space
And free our spirits from the machine and into a divine place.

Once all the pieces start lining up, we will know
That this was the style all along. Head to toe
We are the light powering through the hologram
Now the bodies that lie and feed us into the scam

Of this Earthly plane confusing reality,
Lost in the messes that come from duality
The shade of grey holds no judgments now
Time and space have no relevancy, Ciao!?

That's the program and we are separate from it
Which brings us closer to the absolute ultimate
Truth
That we are immortal consciousness, sharing 3D
Until the fighting ends and we can ascend,
Using our 5th dimensional powers to be
                    All that is in equal amazingness.

As long as reason has reach,
We can correctly assume our futures.
If the stars above are the past
Along with my life in front of me,
Than my futures lies behind me; in the back of my mind.
Endless possibilities connect and
Make ties while creating the people and materials
Needed to construct an earthly continuity.

Using the power of intention,
We sift the light through
And begin climbing the
Rope of manifestation.

Each cell of our consciousness
Mirrored upon the wall of the tunnel
Adjusting our minds to the
Concept of _is_.

Believing in the magic of the moment,
Grants us the creation we aspire to
Bring us all together.

Frustration built from curiosity
Fuels creative problem solving.
It is within deceptions we trail to
The darkness of the lying source.

Underneath the human condition,
Essence of all dictates circumstance
To relax us from programming.

In our natural state we become
Determined to show others love is key

For our sea diving adventures.
Making friends with marine
Dinosaurs who warn of the time Vortex.

The good ol pen and paper distraction.
Like being alone with one's thoughts but
Sending onto the blank legacy for everyone.
Multi-layered existence from a simple stream.
Painting with words

The tug of war between my heart
And mind is mediated by my soul.
Within reason lies instant results, yet
The heart finds the pleasures in a well
Thought out multiple lesson journey
Inside my soul a compromise exists but
Only as energy.
The controller of the body has final say despite all good intuition.
Now we know the physical is a distraction
To the metaphysical and that achieving it
Is to feel and know it as eternal -
Not a prize on a pedestal for one champ only.
I give up my superficial perspectives and
Make room for an energetic lens.
Auras and intentions will mask the traditional looks
For equality to fuel the future.

Step by step
The process of things are slowly realized
Things are not as easily downloaded
As we think them to be now in the speed era.
Going back to that x kb/hour rate
And then to the point where news arrived

Months later.
Let that breath's journey envelop your soul.
It's the most glorious gift we can ask for
In it we will feel we are alone and in company
Complete with love and joy.

Forgiving the rocks and blockages on the air's pathway
We use our courage to clear all that's not needed.
Totally in awe of the moment,
Void of other's energetic fields
Choosing our happiness
Embracing the light
Neutral to the dark
I am cosmic dust with you.

The heart step   vs.
                                                    Feet stepping into
The muck so very similar yet
This is our separation:
Mind and physical --- emotional and metaphysical,
Desire to be an encompassing whole;
   Breaking down the what was to
Make room for what is + can be.
Our dense three dimensional programming
At this point feels so threatened by
Cosmic destiny that it reaps its
own demise.
The strength in survival depends on our
detachment from this realm and realization of
Our shared consciousness transcending to
it's proper home.
   Then can the heart be true, free and
     Unbound from circumstance.

We are the generation of
            LIKE
Because we've forgotten we are
            ALIKE

MMMMMM Close Ur EYES

~~~~~~~~~~~~~~~~~~~
~~~~~~~~~~~~~~~~~~

You'll still see the slit
If you've mastered the clit.

If not () you're stuck in a
Vertical Universe where
Gravity takes control

Shifts---------------------You
                    /   Way |
                              /   / |
              Any------------Which |

     |

              |------------------------------/
              | Except the way you want to go

OH MONEY, YOU SO CRAZY

Oh how I love to rant about money;
It drives people, that's money honey.
Unless of course you let honey fuel you.
It's biodegradable & although it doesn't
Grow on trees. it's bee made

Existence shuns our ignorance and
Glorifies nature's beautiful pattern.

Oh, to see their faces when money is given...
Or taken away.
The power of the bill, the number
Controls the human mind by
Categorizing dreams into $ (dollar signs).

Oh, my fellow earthlings, the material
You seek starts within you.
The tiniest atoms sent out to
The universe of giving lie within your psyche.

Oh, if only you didn't live in dis-ease.
The thoughts that drive you criminally insane
Are impassioned by the false stream of wealth
That numbers, bills and coins promise.

Oh, my brother, the sea of knowledge is gratis
Like the shooting stars, waterfalls and praying mantis.
Life is for loving, learning to do so and teaching others.
We shall be stagnant no longer! Our evolution is calling us
To take charge and start a revolutionary fuss.

Oh, how quiet are your plans
Close your eyes and let the flow of
The wave provide you with joy, understanding & the way.

This is the life that always ends.
It will go on and on my friends.
Some people tell me it gets better
But more later than sooner

I'll be the one telling others it's
        The life that never ends...

The dungeon windows are an escape
For the slaves of the machine.
"How? you ask "if they have an iron drape?"
Because through the darkness there is sunshine.

They gather their star knowledge
By meditation under the sun
Now longing to get out of college
To see the real world and run

Far away and wide
To the western ocean side.
Where the surf will flow
And love can show

You the truth.

Where is the medium? Would I fly away?
Is the pull too strong? But my work here isn't done.
I feel like I am spontaneously combusting back into stardust.

Dark matter takes over me with a solution:
Breathe, re-calibrate, adjust frequencies, trust, become intuition.
Be you. Know it, believe it and don't listen to anyone, including
yourself.
My inner eyesight is a distraction from the
Buzzing interference in the world of old.

Breath, balance, body, spirit.
Memory, knowledge, mind, routine.

Duty, progression, education, career,
Fuel, consciousness, curiosity, questions.
Assumptions, perspectives, pathways,
Decisions, choices, gaining, releasing.
Reaching, wanting, having, earning, sharing.
Giving, being, meditating, fighting, arguing.
Winning, losing, fainting, cheating, creating.
Fucking, manipulating, caressing, uniting,
Diffusing, fantasizing, television, 3D.
Void, light, hole, beating, rising, ripping,
Separating, chakras, nubis, scars,

Filtering the old, leaving only 5D.

Violet flame, steak knives, skinning,
Money, crash, cage, slavery, injustice.
Imbalance, waste, hierarchy, policy.
Dharma, satori, freedom, crashing.
Loneliness, outcast, loser, different, freak,
Weird, bully, group mentality, commune,
Innocence, love family, friends, hugs,
Cuddles, dogs, pets, fun, telepathy.
Empathy, selfishness, wonder, illusions.
Polaroids, albums, frequencies, 528 hz,

Multidimensional cosmic secret agent.

Re-calibrating, room for everyone, light-body.
Dream sky, bridging, smiling, laughter.
Togetherness, dining, adventure, explore.

Natural pace, back to zero point.

The only thing I can truly know is that I
Know nothing at all except we were all

Born of woman, divine female energy,
Kundalini ascension.

29/09/15

In a peaceful place
Where sleep approaches
The Mitote ceases its thunder.

My breath connects with yours
And the pacing shifts
With my focus on stillness.

Silence

A break in time wraps
Our focus into potentiality.
The ladder appears in the mind's eye.

Climbing into true being
Raising our frequency to natural waves
And ascension of light bodies manifests

Energy Surge.

Where do we go from here?
Who's in control?
We are what we think.

Thoughts of what feels right
inside the cosmic database
Reprogrammed into the daily fight

Reemergence
of
Truth.

A breath squeezing in & out,
Life and death at the precipice of my being,
I consider again my
Role in the world vision.

The ego within this time space matrix
Likes to mimic what has already worked before.
We mend the material to fit our skin
In hopes of becoming the greatest.

For those of us outside of this game
We struggle to find the balance of survival.
Tying to be the outreaching hand for our lost friends
While paying the bill for our so called rights.

In the end, it's a test of the mind.
I know for certain I like feeling good and
Like when others to as well.
The transition from individual security to
Unifying love of all is the key to our evolution.

Lightworkers come together to shine purity
Upon the earth and it's dwellers to serve
As a mirror to those lost in the shadows.
Slowly our words, thoughts and actions ripple
Through the 100 monkeys and more questions arise.

What am I living for? Which thoughts merit energy?
Who is this all for?
No longer the 1% but 100 percent of us can out grow
Fear and work for the land of love:
That which most resembles of inner child's innocence,
Our wish for a love reality to begin with.

Relax,
Breathe.
They would order,
Not say.

I govern
Those actions and
I do them
At my own pace.

Do not trust those that say
Relax in a tone not based in
Universal flow-
It's easily manipulated.

I don't point to personalize demons,
For they live in multiple people.
I'm sure these new friends are fine,
In this reality.

Others may not be so lucky.
"All good brother:
Is it? Was it?
Will it be?   *06/2019*

PROSE

10/11/15

Purpose:
The ego's identity crisis.
I AM, I WANT, I NEED, I FEEL – No chance to think.

I am to love. I love therefore I am. I create therefore I have.
To be a son, brother, neighbour, friend, nephew, grandson.
To bring light & love upon the planet. To breathe.

Black holes follow us wherever we go.
They could be ours, theirs or the others, but they will always exist.
What we can change is our proximity to them. We are in charge of how much they govern our lives and how much we allow them to manipulate us.
The darkness is a part of it all.
We are the beacon of light, opposing all malevolent forces.
There is only the existence, the tension is created by us.
Our perspective is what matters

21/10/2015

Maybe its not so much that we have to remember, but that we need to forget.
Let go of the hurt:
Humiliation, shame, guilt, jealousy, anger, all fear and byproducts.
When we laugh together & suddenly forget.

"What were we talking about? Why were we angry? What frustrated us?"
I forget because the laughter was so joyous, so true, so in the one zone of love that anything part of a rational linear timeline becomes irrelevant.
When I become the AWE, I go from lighter to laughter.
We reach the level & become the clean slate we entered as.

CONSCIOUSNESS VS THE PROGRAM

We see it all around us, our other
Senses can confirm it.
One second we are our mother's child,
Then we become society's roles for us: our duty, our purpose, as meant by structure.
The 10 year old behind the wheel does not perceive the same worth as the software. We begin to compare and compartmentalize the pieces of physical realms pretending to have an upper hand in our freedom. In truth, we enslave our inner child to a world foreign to the bounds of a kid's imagination.
This is not the playing field we love.
Thrust into the depths of despair, it is here that nightmares roam to annihilate dreams and fuel the vampires' destiny.

Everyday we write the book to gain a piece of something lost.
When that epiphany of inner trust and self love emerges from within and out to the zen universe, only then can we feel true liberty of a world falsely collaborated in.
Divide from the duality.
Embrace spirituality as the master of your dreams you make the universe flow as she so wishes.
Consciousness works through the system to experience full potential on our manifestation planet. Now it believes it can bring its creations into the core of existence.~~~

We've taken her on an adventure, now she will take us, like the
beginning.

Life Thru Me

                                 makes at my pace
I can choose whichever place   makes me most comfortable. In
control of the moment my feelings, reactions to be of my own
and not that of a button.
Nothing left to materialize on the planet but the essence of anti-
matter, unison of hearts. Tipping point of creation goes back to
inception.
We are the new perception.
Deserts, fields, open nature. Peace of mind.
Diving into the sound wave frequencies mix carbon atoms take
us to the next level of being, leaving gold to shine for eyeful
people.
Prana breath frees me.

It seems the more there is, the less
Room for nothing to exist

To successfully merge in and out of lightbody aka the art we
perfected while sleeping,
To accomplish this would release us from the veil.

In the end it's about how much light/prana/universal
consciousness we let work through us.
Day to day, thought to thought, moment to moment:
Are we accepting the universal truth?

I am a cell of consciousness
I am modelled from the cells before my existence.
My goal is to be less like them and more like me.
As I grow and integrate with other cells I choose the options that will propel me into my best self.
Shedding skin and consciously fasciating a better construct.
What is "better"? - A unified me, happier, confident, powerful-->
but without the need to use it ~ Harmonious~.
Is that not what we all strive for with*in* and with*out.*
In my most pure of essence, this is what helped create me and my original dot.
Light and love is the human translation of that higher vibration.

Our language is vibration.
We are able to feel the range of low to high.
What is the lowest? --> Death, despair, fear, until you enter "unbeing".
Kundalini rising brings us to peace, love, harmony and pure consciousness in forms of laughter, joy, harmony energy. What is the highest? Pure imaginative being? In that space are we superhuman? Can we be all? Bring all into existence that can be? Now, once we're set in a frequency, other like cells will be around, able to exchange, observe, exist together, organize. Why?--> To grow in size; the larger the amount of cells on one level the more important, celf confident, safe, sustained, guarded, one feels as an individual and group. ...Until..

Rogues <---><<--->
In either direction, Because they can--To try a new level, test limits, rebel.
So from there the same stages occur... <(O)> cycle - recycle
Positively charged rogue cells vs Negatively charged rogue cells
Each searching for a way to innovate their existence; one to achieve a "new low", the other

"an improved high" --> each striving for satisfaction.
They both could play at the expense of the other, individual morals vary.
Some could argue on both sides that they are doing it for the better of the majority.
Key difference--> Acceptance and understanding that One is part of the Whole.
My pain is your pain so I should no longer inflict pain.
Rogues will fail for they lack the support of the ultimate life force, fuel of All That Is.

The World will revolve, no matter what.
Things will happen
Ego & Kundalini will find actions.

Constant flow on involution & evolution battling
It's not good vs. evil; this is a story of inside vs. outside.

Reshaping the ego is traumatic, like the world crashing in on itself.
All we know are the things we've been through and learned from sense experience.
Those ego moments where it seems like its okay to dip into the physical - I must detach.
I'm not here to indulge. When opportunities arise I assess importance. Do I need it? The key is not to
go out of my way to find it / focus my attention on getting it.

We feel claustrophobic because the ego mind says I deserve to have lots of comfortable space, but we are not

physical beings, in each other's ways, we're a bunch of floating atoms.
As adults we forget how we perceived as children: Everything new in the moment.
We get older and repeat, tricking ourselves into blind perception. The mind is the one confused with the mantra and the exploration that we are not the body.
We only understand: we are the body, confusion ensues to ego, mind & spirit.
Yes I have a body, Yes I have a soul, Yes my soul governs my body, Yes my higher self will direct my body through sadhana to a balanced unity between both realms.

I am the effervescent light source in the Now.
The power of the moment fuels all good intentions.
I rely on universal love consciousness within me to move forward.
All love in my life is a Reflection of my beacon.
Anxieties are a disconnect from presence.
I am all in the moment, peace of mind.
The healing power of the universe is innate. It is meant to regenerate life.
We can send our energy to the past, present or future with positivity
We aim to ease pain not create anxiety as we in our ego minds tend to do.

If I were to sum up some goals that tie into the global vision and my life review, it would be the integration of dream consciousness to earthly life.
Bringing dream sky over our heads,
Bridging dream bodies with the earth,
Blowing out love and light, harmony, joy and laughter at the core of all.

My satisfaction lies in my level of honesty within the moment;
I don't always have to be Mr. Smiles but in the lover zones I will be
Honest and continue to contribute to the light grid.

Simple pleasures, especially in material terms, are great but
They shouldn't be perceived as the end all be all of happiness in that moment.
Those dependencies become addictions.
The way out is to detach from it and find there is no void inside because that is where light and
Dark meet within us. It is our yin yang and it's perfect.
When we live to satisfy different chakras, we must take is as a journey to a lesson and not the one to end all.

Perhaps we want an easy switch, or the challenge,
We're all gradually moving upwards anyway.
The most significant changes happen within us first and from that
Outwardly over our Venus project to overtake a system inundated by heavy metals.

December 17th 2016

The veil of illusions is kicking off it's last legs.
Human consciousness mixed in with the old are in conflict.
The love beings and "untouched" ones (those separated from old beliefs and new technological digital identities)
are bringing in the new dream.

The chalice is now strong enough to withhold these energies and the Dream Bridge to Rainbow World is making progress.

Grid Changes:

This filter reflects layers upon layers of lightwork re-calibration.
As the light vibrations resonates closer to earth than ever before,
we're experiencing bursts of love energy.
Much like the polar vortex of weather, the grid works similarly:
The longer the distance between similar temperatures, the
greater the momentum to increase or decrease in size.
The "landing" or descent of light allows new weather patterns
to form, fix and adjust until down becomes up.

Ego & the sense of accomplishment:

Of course we want to fly on the heels of self pride; growing up,
idolatry was all around us.
Somewhere in the screens and reflections we lost sight of why
we wanted purpose:
To reconnect with all that is to let go of selfish feats.

We wanted to be high like those we looked up to so that we too
could glide on a cloud.
Forget the money, legacy, ownership.
Just be in the greatest potential, be a role model for light warriors,
detaching from the I AM, I Do, I've Done to the
WE ARE!

SPIRIT

Love all around
 Inside and out
  Our true selves
   Emerge from the grotto

        Release from the chains
        With your heart
         The key has been
         Locked in a safe

          This whole time
          When you thought
           Helplessness was all
          Now you see

           Feel the light
           Lifting you up
            Clearing the clouds
             Freedom for the fallen

To find peace, one must seek their spiritual home;

There lies a base of energy that can be tapped into
At all times and spaces.

Upon re-energizing, the body, mind and spirit unite
Like business people at a meeting, to share their ideas &
Aspirations until they meet again.

Every moment there is a lifetime where you can travel anywhere.
However, when your mind is made up,
Your body is grounded and your soul is free.
You must return.
You must learn.

Thinking 2 much about
What could happen
Stalls anything from
Happening

We are always one with consciousness
And the River of Time flows
Always with God
The highest.

Awe, Yes, The Saviour
The individual who mirrors the Great One in the sky.
Doesn't it suck that of the billions of earthlings
The only hope and guidance we find is from personalized idols?

Change your channel and you might enjoy the silence of static.
You might just find God Within U.

The moons pass on a legacy of human corruptions,
But we shall awaken when our brothers and sisters from
Niburu guide us across the channel and into the
Deep Cove of Truth and understanding,
Unity and plurality of sense.

Dream to infinity and colour your path
Into the deep beyond.
The wild calls for you glory and skill.

Hold their hands and surge the light.
Blood only feels better when it flows
Bright.

On an unknown date, in an unknown land
A fly whizzes across the sky.
Knowing only instinct, it uses a special tool
Used in all life called imagination.

From the tiniest to the hugest,
Things carry on with thought.
There can be great dangers ahead,
That which the pain body longs for

As the mind collects pieces to create
A full existence, the spirit, equally in
Love and hate of death, evolves
7.5 billion humans, trillions of animals and
Insects and plants can't be wrong.

The faded pencil
Works still
You hear the words
            until
It ranges in size
to its demise
And left to be a stump

Solar eclipse to the chest
Rays penetrate shadows
And the darkness is uplifted.
Minutes of pain washed by rains of redemption.
A new start is granted for everyone.

But, with simple dark magick all
Can go back to what it was.

Live always, consciousness rules.
This vacation from hell is a gift
To maintain its glory we must choose
The Heart
The Dwelling of birth and death
To overcome the ego's obsession with destruction.

Time: the illusionary master, can bring us
Hope or wipe it away completely.

To let go
          Release
               Relinquish
Say our last goodbyes to the
Things that have stalled us.
We recognize the difference between
Being grounded and choose
The Heart's path.
Growing into the higher self
Requires dedication to the Whole
We are what we do and we do
What we believe is truth.

The spinning Earth;
A somber setting
For natural beats
To unravel.

Somewhere within time
A Heart skips a rock
And rather enjoys the spontaneity.

Beings all around
Become influenced by the
Consciousness of surprise.

Intuition still holds key but
Control now finds home in each mind.
Nature fins passion,
Behind this new rhythm.

But now full swing creation
Needs a wiser discipline

From the stars comes a warm light
Mother and Father together in harmony
Gather the family of truth
For the dinner of champions.

The Rules of western society dictate our lives:
My category restricts but I'm still doomed
To be what you and they wish to see.
Even if I shine like gold, don't label me
I'm out of the mould like my starseed siblings
Living to change, rebel and expel as much light
As we can to avoid a growing fight
Between dualities so sure they will survive.
Yes, I want love and a career to fulfill my purpose
However it will not define me.
It is my knighthood and leadership that lights paths
Bringing the new map to the people.
Its my heart and passion either way
I open my arms to have any and all join me in
Soaking up the sunshine.
If one body can commit that I will dub her queen
Until then the war goes on and I will be me

To the highest frequency
Dreaming and fulfilling.

Chained to the now
I used to think how
And the other words too
Until I stopped to become new
As it was every once in awhile
Every time I shared a smile
Glorious light filled my soul
As I go with the ball & roll

The Great Silence
  The Harmony of Breath
So many take for granted.
It's a coming back to source we must
appreciate.
We are source; zero point. And breath is
consciousness
This deep oblivion of all that is
Clears vocabulary, action and setting
 to be it's self
    The ever wondrous existence
    Clean slates, blackness reaches for light
And we collide our particles to
Accelerate manifestation
    Vibration in sound and light make the present
    We are only the moment;
    The moment: US.

If the reality we dwell was
Written in pen,
Couldn't the realm we wish become real?

By means of ink? Or on a screen?
Perhaps written in the sand?

The sand of time would be a powerful tool,
If we could wrap our hands around ti.
Every time we try,
Time keeps slipping
Through our fingers.

We may panic for a moment,
Until we realize that we are standing
On the beach with the ocean wide ahead and
All we really need,
Lies within our reach.

My magic hands guide me to the stage.
Life lights in time space are so powerful,
I channel the intensity to my fellow Countrymen.

Our hearts now artistically combine
For a festival of humanitarian
Beauty and salvation.

She's getting closer to the truth.
She doesn't understand the tunnel is long
And branches to other realms.

She prepares for the earthly fight.
Is she ready?

The last blood determines the century.
Bleed for peace.

PURPOSE

A full circle of hope,
The steam of mistakes
Disintegrates.

I jump in patiently
Like lightning in the sea,
I arrive full force.

Upon re-learning & experiencing,
I have connected with my surrounding.

The love we have to give is plenty.

I am here as I hug and kiss the base.
There are any games but it's not a race.

The Purpose ignites your light
It brings us higher.

I pray
The day

Has arrived:
The Music & Movement
        of the Moment
            Are at One.

Along the path of gold,
Light surrounds for the most part and
Darkness lurks at a safe distance.

My steps are directed through the sunshine
By the warm hands that shaped me,
Until my curiosity pulls my focus.

Leaving me free to explore
With others in my environment
Who came from different beginnings.

Now I must learn, grow & evolve
With the knowledge I gain from my senses
As I try to remain my self.

Identity, still weak, struggles
To maintain the roots of my family tree
That guides me to my most complete being.

Broken free and more in control,
I see all that glitters is not gold.
Perhaps I was misled by a world of grandeur.

The land of Oz isn't beyond a
Yellow brick road of royalty
But rests in the clicking of our heels.

For there is no place like home
To feel complete & wrapped in love
While the unpredictable forest
Mourns the soul of a fallen tree.

Time now wanders around the playground,
Lost in the transition to adulthood.

Everyone depended on this wonder kid for so long,
Now he's an afterthought to the dreamsky.

Who knew that his very advantage would be his demise,
The stretching of space is so yester-something.

He'll join Father Sky & they'll bond over
Sharing their first names in books.

The evidence that what was once worked
And did not work for the mechanics of the well thought out

Blueprints of cosmic nature.

Our patterns show spontaneity and awe,
Those calendar boxes kept the light out.

Time to step up and embrace
The brilliant truth of existence.

A life without wilted skins & decaying organs.
Instruments to measure tickity tock vanish.

We're left with one another,
The most important piece of being.

Pineal

Take the outer as it's been.
The source of weird but oh so marvellous.
Stories and imagination fuel dreams,
Creating balance between realities.

Lodged in the inner,
We are the varieties of the
Universe and we can
Flutter shades.

Separation of Space-Time-
I refuse to care.
I no longer need to be me.
My obligations remain loyal to
All Energy,
Free to be spirit in & out of human realms.

The eyes closed world
Rainbow city in my 3rd eye
Bridging dimensions with our hearts
The beats emit light shock-waves.

Aliens in houses above our heads
Plan a master takeover of our bodies.
This invasion will be our blessing
For the pains of the 9-5 slavery.

The Not World DisOrder will falter

And the truth about our power as
Love and light beings will set us
Free for the first time in thousands of years.

Newest children to the Earth
Bring space rocks from other dimensions
To heal the hearts of the mortal ill.
They carry potions made of intention
And cast their spells with smiles
And glowing eyes.
Take the gazer into the outer to
Reveal the inner conflicts and
When the smoke clears and the mirror
Reveals itself we can mold the
Imperfections of our journeys to follow
The future of our destined self
And unite the indigo for their
Rightful kingdom will be declared upon them.

Cosmos unite to dance
With mortals
If they can handle it
There can be explosive results.
A realm dedicated to intertwined
Energy, everlasting in our veins
Drinking from the spiked punch
The weak will falter and dream
Only to return to their moments
of Redemption.
All for a chance at something new
Where breath is master and
All is within wind.
Light beings carried by truth and wisdom.

It appears as though the planets
Are the true culprits
Of my limbo feeling,
Nerves to the ceiling
With my acceptance and serenity
I have come closer to my destiny.

Belief and scale in power
Behind a star that will shower
Radiation transforming into crystal fate
Bring my year strength or so they speculate.

I will continue my growth in peace
Way longer than my signed lease
For the story is constantly changing
But passion, love and utopia will be charging
The light in the global fight.

Cross-dimensional existence
Annihilates games of gain.
Indigo stripped screens
Mesh to the outskirts of the cosmic farmlands
Dusting the fertile zone
Brought us History, turning
To blippery boop
All words disintegrate to pure un-
Judged mint day.

Waves of colour sweep into our souls
We let it penetrate and manipulate our holes
Until we focus and take control of certain emotions
We don't want getting tossed into the oceans.

Sea salt extracts our negativity slowly
So that on Sunday we can feel more holy.
It's the restart button for our stress
But the beach won't clean up our mess.

The efforts of our raison d'etre like sand
Passing through glass and into my hand
A certain evolution in our body's electromagnetic field
Will give us the power to shield
All unnecessary nonsense
Into the past tense.

24/11/13

Eager
     Jumping Beans
                       Excited
                            Cafe has
welcomed them. What next? we love,
we play back and forth but the
field changes
    No longer can they do as they please
  Electric fences border them,
They can work for their ~

Playing in the fields of colourful existence
Breaking through to the absolute sustenance
That which is all indeed has all paths
And the connecting essence of source
Makes for the journey's pure life
Taking in the New Earth by the horns
The unfortunate ones still within duality pray
For their individuality to carry on since
They believe it is their accomplishment
We send our love and hope that they may join

the collective accomplishment of our Race
The Earth life manifestations:
That which came from nothing;
The miracle of our entire reality

Awakening in the depths
We've reached the final steps
More confusing than ever but so powerful
What are we to do in these final hours?
                          PUSH, add force
Join the wave consciously as it tumbles over
this matrix and into the old earth.
Bringing us to the Venus love, recoiled solo
Hearts imploding; the pressure intensifies
So many colours whistling around trying to
find the whirlpool to disperse itself
Pallets of our identities re-imagine our beings

Shared space, selfish time
The battle of our beings
Lost in an alternate universe
A mission being seeded as we dream.
Those ultra dimensional experiences
Thrust us to and fro from the old to
the new and back again.
Forced every morning as we wake up to remember
and forget, learn and unlearn once more
Until collectively we shatter the makeshift
Reality that vampires from space designed
to feed themselves.
We are the light beings of the future
Our stars shining light years around
Brought to you by the choices of the present
Based upon the mistakes of our past

This is where we need to be.
Here is the place we think the now into existence,
There can only be one zero point
And it lives in the collective heart.
Feeding our power to co-exist.

Dream to infinity and colour your path
Into the deep beyond.
The wild calls for your glory and skill.

Hold their hands and surge the light.
Blood only feels better
When it flows bright.

Using the power of intention,
We sift the light through
And begin climbing the rope of manifestation.

Each cell of our consciousness
Mirrored upon the walls of the tunnel
Adjusting our minds to the concept of is.

Believing in the magic of the moment
Grants us the creation we inspire to
Bring us all together.

Revolutionizing
Re-calibration, Re-frequensizing, Re-Assesing
Trapped in a code, What's the way out? Freedom of the mind
Discipline of the spirit, master of the body.
This is not about taking them down.
This is about bringing us up.

05/08/2016

Shining ball of energy, crackling,
Sparks fly in all directions
Masters of time and space tone it down to a
Comfortable level. Light show
Back in the body's mind, we try to connect the dots.
Simply put, I am an animal.
On a more complicated level I am a highly energetic
Being from space trying to filter my power into a DNA
Program created for enslavement.
What is right: bliss or shame, ecstasy or regret?
Delight or Denial?
I am satori in motion, a caged orgasm.
Can it ever be black & white?
Will the juice change into drinking water...
Does my crystallization frost the world...
What is my sexual purpose?
I'll never be normal
Where do I go now?

17/12/15

A free love movement shifts our level,
Keeps some stagnant and rocky.
Where would the 3D end & 5D start?
Other than the obvious climaxing of our perspectives.

Do we use this commune as a rehab from
Our addiction to the shaping dimension,
Or could this be our pseudo enlightenment
Camp for the spiritually confused?

If I really want a group of lovers,
Feeling the moment as one breeze,

I must renounce my sense of nerve ending
Pleasure and fully embrace chakral satori.

My seeds will be recycled for a parallel
World of expectations of manifestation;
That which we've left behind at the
Gates of pure love & blissful smoke swapping.

Had enough of playing your role,
I'm not the man of your dreams,
I can't be your saviour
And in return I'll try not to find in you
The one who can make my dreams come true.

All we can hope for is believing in the truth,
One moment, one spirit, one world.
Free of expectation, void of paper prints.

I'm not the system and I'm free of pain.
So don't make me the one to blame,
When the tears smudge notes in your script,
Just remember noone bought your pitch.

There is no crew or budget,
You are the universe you're fighting against
Fighting for and looking to for love.

Once you let go of the need of others,
Bright lights will keep you warm
And angels will be by your side
To caress the bumps and calm the tide.

LIGHTWORK

His Army answers to a higher power
When it comes to witching hours.
They aren't a part of his team,
Only the devil's dream.

A legacy of evil and corruption
Will lead to a global eruption.
Love will conquer & they will leave.
Hopefully they won't receive
Parting gifts from the 1%
Or I will have to do more than vent
Through my words in ink
To end the wretched stink.

If you had a "super power" what would it feel like?
Energy coarsing thru the body.
Where does it go, what does it look like coming out?

I am a lightworker; my weapons are
Smiles, laughs, words, hugs, kisses,
Meditations, mantras, movement.

Inhaling & exhaling all that is and
Aspires to be the greatest potential.
If there is a Utopian universe parallel,
We see it and breathe it
In & out
Integrating it with our reality, our perspectives, our dreams.

The Slinky Philosophy:

The balance of Light
Shakes from right to left.

Waves of rainbow
Crash into your flow

Your phalanges dance
With the array of power

White light in dark hands.

The genie has the consciousness
To keep everyone happy

So he gives them the power of light

But the man gives them something more distracting...

`~~A Slinky~~`

GUATEMALA 2009

Lightworkers unite and free the
Beings of their slave games
Their chains shall no longer belong to them but
Their masters' reincarnates.
May balance and wholeness be with you all.

A shift in humanity's laws
Will show us our flaws

Of the past.
We must act fast.

Creation is the key
And always has been.
For the universe can see
What it takes to win.

Our hearts will unite
                and fight
For all that is right.

We will sing, dance & perform
Upon Mother Nature's storm.
She will rejuvenate,
We will celebrate.

A connected world
That began with one word:
Love

Magical humanity,
In perfect insanity,
Harmoniously rejoice
And use their voice
To unite the notes &
Set sail on boats
Of the master fusion.

The political landscape mirrors our own planetary
Alignments & calls for the gathering of energies to
Pull together in the transport to the higher dimensions.

As we trust & love more, so will honesty in our hearts
Change the way we work together.
The family will once again be joined in harmony.

Romantic love stays caught in the webs
As the lightworkers step aside from the mission
For a cigarette break.
In the meantime,
We take few chances and sometimes forget that
Movement is love and not the other way around.

His last candle can't take the cold of lost thought and
succumbs to darkness,
Embracing movement as sexually as he can until the thirst of
Another gently squeezes through to prove her dedication to
salvation.

In my soul there is a light
Within that light there is a world
For all the cherries to grow.

Far deep in the hearts of our
Lost loves there lies a tree
Of endless beauty.

As a child to his mother we are shamed by
Guilt.
With you infinite wisdom
You will make all tears melt.

The magnetic field envelops & tugs
Us into a similar frequency.
My breeze turned into a wind, then a storm.
But only one drop was needed for all to manifest.

Lightworkers, move to the beat
Of the drum of life.
We float along the light
Towards the bounce of sound.

Take hold of the rope
For the moment to ground is now.
Just as it was before
In the loop of time wars.

Shine bright as you descend
But dim accordingly for
Your mask won't be seen by everyone
And anonymity is a fool's game.

Engage in the earthly spirit,
Tie your heart to the strings of the strong,
Intertwine the songs of the un-defeat-able,
Inflate the balloon of progress.

The skyway to our highest self
Lies beyond your calcified being,
So free your matrix of deceit and
Rejoice with the swing of nature.

Rainbow world awaits the invasion of
Lonely hearts and true believers
Carry the flame with those you love
Bring back the fire that ignited Atlantis.

The cries of the Earth
Awaken the warriors for the drill.
Their training will now be put to the test
As their destinies take flight.

Energy sources are a gift
Which we have taken for granted
So we must ask for Her forgiveness
And fight for all life.

In honor of the magic inside,
We stand for a future that represents
Our dreams & the beauty we know
As we relinquish greed and embody selflessness.

How far are we willing to go?
The morality that brought us here
May have to be sacrificed for the greater good
Or perhaps we can keep our hands clean
Enough to not dig a deeper hole.

———

The Two Earths finding space to share,
In a zone where one is frantic
The other calm as her lakes.
Is an interesting episode in our long story.

I close my eyes and the bridge is closer
Than the previous moments.
Others may not perceive it so but in me
It's plain to see Wave X is our new stratosphere.

Every breath is like a baby's first steps
As we enter a room where earthlings have never been
And where the earth was too young to remember
The exhilarating energy and sparkling wallpaper.

We have a textbook for this class
However, the pages are blank and our
Fingers are made of pens, markers and paintbrushes
To leave an explanation to others of this collage.

We're to embrace the gift of this moment
With full gratitude since past, present and future
Happen simultaneously for our education.
Now we can learn and grow without deadlines or in boxes.

The group project is our syllabus,
Our marks are graded by our light.
Teachers & student unite
For the entry exam into 5D.

21/09/2015

Painting our reality
With a new brush
And vibrant colour
To take the wind
By the tails &
Reshape the clouds.

The resistance exists
To keep us aware
That the fight isn't over
Until truth is overwhelming
Our hearts into pure love.

Sometimes easy to remember,
Mostly; easier to forget.
In the end, our purpose collides
With highest intentions & uniting intuition.

20/10/15

Riding the wind of true essence
Unleashing power from all we feel
Into the Earth and out to beyond.

Heart strings wrap around me like silk
Making contact with breath as physical lines blur
Without stirring the pot.

Feeling true to our existence and
Enveloping love and light's potential
For the harmonization of beings.

29/10/15

World War 3
Was quiet for some.
Battles in all dimensions
Taught us a millennia of knowledge
On how to be.

Now we pick up pieces
Of lost hearts and spirits
To unite the energy of a
World filled with truth
As we establish a new platform
For our existence.

ALBY'S GENIUS

Formulas for ascension
Fail to produce scientific results.
In the union of our souls,
Number and letters blur.

Somewhere in between you may find
The genius of our time explain that
Love energy is the strongest and
Most powerful force in the universe.

All parasitical annoyances scramble
To survive in the light and most
Find solace in the human shadow,
Weak at the promise of individuality.

The ego knows the truth
Yet those bugs seep into the matrix
To fool even the lightest of humanity
For the glory of having a meaningful story.

In the end, voices and emotions constantly
Fight against them to reflect purity
Of the moment and absolution of fear,
Bringing us closer together.

Back to zero point,
Perfection insists on beauty
Through the atoms that make us
The most seamless of illusions.

COSMIC

Cloudy skies are more like twisted smoke rings
Blowing out from Heaven's lungs and formed
By the highest mouth.

Pain pours down and soaks the third.
We hear the screams of the past and dimensional
Woes of the future.

Joys of our youth become trapped behind the glass doors.
Those who believe in burdens remain silhouettes.
I can phaze through, but can't bring others along.

When the sky clears there may be hope
But one should never be fooled by illusions.
Sunshine starts from within and relfects out.

The dream plane has room for all our stars,
We shant let the 1 control the map.
Taking our love beyond the heights of structural shame
Will set the clock to one: our natural divine timing.

Stars made of inc & graphite

--(the new lead)

~~~~~~~~~~~~~

Fade on paper

Their cousins in the sky
Although they too die,
~~~~~~~~~~~~~

Have a deeper existence
For life is born under them.

The magic of the night sky in
A painting can ignite thought +
                    curiosity.

But our dreams are in the cosmos
And we have to believe that
They are brightening our path.

The pages may be really light,
To be used for white balance.
However they are man made
Far away from getting laid.
All they care about is getting paid
Enough to vacation and pay the maid.

Back to the stars
Pluto, Mars, Saturn & Mars
The true heroes of our earth
Who fought in myth & defended honour.

They are lost in time and space
Brethren to our flashing lights in the heavens
And anti-matter to the ******************
                    ****

Inside numbers fluctuate.
Today I started by grounding,
Did this influence the stats?
Is it all determined by cosmic weather?

When the heat is on it feel
Sometimes as I have no choice.

Now in the fluff I am fluid,
Part of everyone and thing.
Choosing neutrality and oneness
Being as authentic as possible.
I am not the astro program,
I have denied the code.

My lessons & essence are
Thoroughly filtered into the stargate of Love.
I must choose the path of evolutionary grandeur.
Our glowing light needs fuel
While the power grid electrocutes the willing.

After all, this shared plane influences us all.
Pulsing through our veins.
We deserve the most thrilling of trips
As atoms that expel into the cosmos
A powder transcending us unto the new highway.

The slaves strategize underneath
Apt weather conditions.

Freedom doesn't guarantee bliss,
Some stay behind.

Truth falls down and cleanses
Open spirits.

Another temporary escape,
Senses distracted for so long.

We've seen too much,
Demanding the world the way it rests in our palms.

Rebellion takes a slight majority,
Silent battles have worn out.

Submission, omission, oblivion,
Our ignorance shields vampire lust.

05/2019

Master plans,
Destinies,
Dreams and Nightmares.
What is ambition when life and death are at stake

The energy demon lurks in the lake,
Subject to the majority.
If chaos is requested -
The wishes come to light.

Appease the beast and
All will be smooth.
No one is to blame,
Turn fear into trust

05/2019

The world is my oyster
The oyster is in a tank,
The tank, in a cell
On your mother-ship

Making lemons with lemonade
Genetically modified existence,
Sunshine created with movie lights

06/2019

The Maya keeps us smiling.

Stand in line,
Pick up your cheque.
Beauty must be real,
In tangible timelines.

Crash and burn,
Let us all collapse.
Sleep on it,
Reset to feed the fishes.

The breath reminds us of the
Uncertainty of structure.
Predictability is shattered,
Energy manifest outside of time & space.
In french we say "time"
For weather, is it not?
Does all not separate based on
Perceptions of high -low
Side to side of systems
Brought out from the seas,
Moved by the moon and
Thrust by atmosphere?
We are Now.
We are the seasons in a breeze
Our hearts beat to the Rays' dance.

GLOSSARY

Ascension: Process of enlightenment of the dense body experience into higher consciousness. Transmutation of density.

Divine Timing: The confident belief that all passes through at once therefore planned within a universal love frequency.

DreamSky: Realm of harmony and peace. Established plane of oneness, truth and serenity.

Stargate: Time/Space re-creation opportunity; window of self destiny.

Zero-point: Culmination of a moment, point from which all connects.

Chakras: Energy vortexes of different vibration, colour, frequency, desire, intention.

Grid: Energy highway connecting intention, will, desire and action. Middle ground between Earth & the Akashiks.

Shakti: Energy highways in and on the body

Light work/er: Energetic alchemy/ist transmuting harm into harmony

Mantra: Repetitions of words including meaning or intention; spell

Mitote: Outside noise, the storm of thoughts before the calm in meditation / mindfullness.

Niburu: Planet X, Idea that a planet that rotates around the galactic sun and enters different solar systems, off setting the established status quo and forcing a reset of ideals.

Nubis: Energy points scattered on and in the body.

Fasciating: Creating fascia, moulding nothing into something.

Sadhana: Personal Spiritual habit, ritual, routine, practice, effort

Biography

Born & raised in Montreal, Anthony's Italian background mixed with the mostly English / French linguistic influence of the multicultural cosmopolitan city launched him into diverse journeys around the world living through varying perspectives.

His need to express himself and transcend his spiritual quest manifested in writing, singing and acting.

While travelling and reconnecting at home, Anthony continues his love of writing & film-making in both documentary & fiction with never-ending dreams of global spiritual unity.